For Raquel—I'm literally Mexican because of you—TB

For Diamela—te quiero abuelita—MJ

PENGUIN WORKSHOP
An Imprint of Penguin Random House LLC, New York

Visit us online at www.penguinrandomhouse.com.

Library of Congress Cataloging-in-Publication Data is available upon request.

ISBN 9780593224496 (pbk)   10 9 8 7 6 5 4 3 2 1 HH
ISBN 9780593224502 (hc)   10 9 8 7 6 5 4 3 2 1 HH

Lettering by Comicraft
Book design by Jay Emmanuel

This is a work of nonfiction. All of the events that unfold in the narrative
are rooted in historical fact. Some dialogue and characters have been fictionalized
in order to illustrate or teach a historical point.

For more information about your favorite historical figures, places, and events,
please visit www.whohq.com.

A WHO HQ GRAPHIC NOVEL

Who Was the Voice of the People?

CESAR CHAVEZ

by Terry Blas
illustrated by Mar Julia

Penguin Workshop

Introduction

Cesar Chavez was born on March 31, 1927, just outside Yuma, Arizona. His family lived in the Sonoran Desert on a ranch, which was bought by his grandparents, Mama Tella and Papa Chayo. They emigrated from Mexico to the United States in 1898. Papa Chayo died before Cesar was born, and Cesar spent his early childhood living with Mama Tella, his parents, Librado and Juana, and his siblings, Richard, Librado, Vicki, and Rita. Cesar's grandmother lived in the main adobe house, while Cesar's family lived in a small cottage on the main ranch. Together, the family worked on tending the land: feeding the animals, collecting eggs, and hauling water to the house.

Cesar didn't like school because the other kids made fun of the color of his skin. The teacher would punish him for speaking Spanish by hitting him on the knuckles with a ruler. He wanted to go outside and kick off his shoes. In class, he wanted to sit with his sister, but the teacher wouldn't allow it because boys were supposed to sit together, separate from the girls.

When Cesar was twelve, his family lost their ranch because of the Great Depression. They had to relocate to California, where there was more work in the fields of the farms. Cesar began working in the fields with his father and noticed what horrible conditions many had to suffer through. A lot of farmworkers worked long hours in the sun with very little pay, no bathrooms, and no meal breaks.

Cesar was heavily influenced by his mother, who ran the household and didn't condone any fighting among her children. But at a young age, Cesar became interested in the teachings of Mahatma Gandhi, a political leader who used nonviolent protest to lead India to independence from Britain. Gandhi's teachings greatly inspired Cesar—he also wanted to create change for farmworkers and his community in a peaceful way.

As he continued to witness the injustices done to farmworkers of many different races and ages, he decided to create a union—a group organized to protect workers' rights. The group called itself the National Farm Workers Association (NFWA). This angered many farm owners and companies who sold fruit and vegetables, especially grapes. One such company was Schenley Industries, which owned a few wineries and vineyards in California. Many migrant farmworkers labored at these vineyards under very poor conditions, struggling in the heat and unable to be part of a union.

In September 1965, the members of Cesar's union began to strike and started picketing at vineyards. They began to make signs and refused to work. But Cesar knew this wasn't enough. Something more had to be done.

DELANO, CALIFORNIA. 1965: NATIONAL FARM WORKERS ASSOCIATION MEETING

IT'S TIME.

WE NEED TO GET THE NUMBERS UP.

CESAR MENTIONED STUDENTS. CIVIL RIGHTS GROUPS. CHURCHES. WE NEED TO REACH OUT TO THEM AND GET MORE PEOPLE TO JOIN THE CAUSE.

HOPEFULLY GAIN SOME MORE RECRUITS FROM THESE GROUPS.

I'LL START MAKING SOME CALLS.

MEXICO

LET'S KEEP UP THE MOMENTUM. THERE'S TOO MUCH AT STAKE. STRIKERS ARE RISKING THEIR JOBS AND THEIR SAFETY. JUST YESTERDAY, SOME FARM OWNERS SPRAYED PICKETERS WITH POISONOUS CHEMICALS.

ROBERTO BUSTOS

6

DOLORES HUERTA

THERE'S ALSO THE BUSINESS OF THE POLICE. THEY INSPECTED OUR CREDIT UNION WITHOUT A WARRANT TO TRY AND FIND SOMETHING TO BLAME ON US. THEY SEEM ON EDGE. THANKFULLY, TODAY WE HAVEN'T HAD ANY INCIDENTS.

WE'LL SEE HOW LONG THAT LASTS.

NO KIDDING. THEY DID NOTHING ABOUT THE MAN WHO DROVE A CAR INTO THE STRIKERS, AND THE ATTACKS WE'VE EXPERIENCED AT THE VINEYARDS OWNED BY SCHENLEY INDUSTRIES HAVE GONE UNINVESTIGATED.

CESAR CHAVEZ

HELLO, EVERYONE.

7

8

CESAR, DELANO TO SACRAMENTO... THAT'S 245 MILES.

I THINK ALL THE PESTICIDES FROM THE GRAPES ARE AFFECTING YOUR BRAIN.

WHAT WE ARE DOING IS GOOD, BUT THE MORE ATTENTION WE CAN BRING TO THE CAUSE, THE BETTER. THE MORE PEOPLE WHO KNOW ABOUT US, THE MORE SUPPORT WE ARE LIKELY TO GET. THIS COULD DO THAT FOR US. IT'S GOOD TO WORK HARD, BUT IT'S BETTER TO WORK SMART.

JUST THINK ABOUT IT.

YOU KNOW THIS IS HAPPENING, RIGHT? HE'S MADE UP HIS MIND.

OF COURSE I DO. IT'S JUST CRAZY ENOUGH THAT IT MIGHT WORK.

MEXICO

13

15

NFWA Flag

In a theater in Fresno, California, at the first convention of the National Farm Workers Association, union members revealed their new flag. They displayed a red banner with a black eagle, its wings spread, over a white circle. Each color has a specific meaning. Black was meant to represent the hard life the farmworkers had to endure. Red was for the many sacrifices they would have to make, and white was for hope.

Cesar asked his brother Richard Chavez and his cousin Manuel Chavez to come up with a symbol that would be easy to recreate. Something anyone could make. They went with the eagle because of its importance to the Mexican flag and Mexican culture. The eagle was a bold, graphic shape—its wings mimicking the shape of Mesoamerican temples and pyramids.

"A symbol is an important thing," Cesar said. "That is why we chose an Aztec eagle. It gives pride. When people see it, they know it means dignity. To me, it looks like a strong, beautiful sign of hope."

18

20

LATER...

HOW LONG ARE YOU GOING TO KEEP US HERE? IT'S BEEN HOURS NOW.

AS LONG AS IT TAKES. I DON'T GOT ANYWHERE TO BE.

THIS COULDN'T HAVE ANYTHING TO DO WITH THE FACT THAT IF A BUNCH OF FARMWORKERS MARCH OUT OF DELANO, THE FARM OWNERS MIGHT GET SOME UNWANTED ATTENTION?

SOME BAD PRESS?

YOU DON'T HAVE A PERMIT FOR THIS PARADE. UNLESS YOU HAVE A PERMIT, YOU MAY AS WELL TURN RIGHT BACK AROUND AND GO HOME.

22

The March from Delano to Sacramento

One of the most crucial moments of the Delano Grape Strike was a march from the city of Delano in Southern California up to Sacramento, which is California's capital city. The distance between the two cities is about 245 miles, but rather than walking directly to Sacramento, the marchers felt they should visit towns and farms along the way to get more farmworkers to join their cause.

As the number of marchers grew, many things needed to be taken into account, such as food, water, bathroom breaks, and sleeping accommodations. This made the march 340 miles long. Eventually, they went through 53 towns and stayed overnight in half. Some of the other towns they visited and passed through were: Richgrove, Ducor, Terra Bella, Porterville, Lindsay, Farmersville, Visalia, Dinuba, Reedley, Sanger, and Selma.

SACRAMENTO

MODESTO

FRESNO

CUTLER

CALIFORNIA
US
99

NFWA

DELANO

28

30

33

35

WELCOME, CESAR. I'M JULIO. I'M IN CHARGE OF THE COMMITTEE FOR THE LOCAL CHAPTER OF THE UNION.

PLEASURE, JULIO.

WE HAVE SOME NEWS. GOOD NEWS.

WE'VE JUST RECEIVED A DELIVERY.

A COMPANY IN LOS ANGELES HAS DONATED OVER ONE HUNDRED PAIRS OF BOOTS TO YOU. EVERYONE WILL GET NEW SHOES TOMORROW.

THAT'S TERRIFIC!

ARE YOU SERIOUS?

I DIDN'T MEAN TO OVERHEAR, BUT DID YOU SAY EVERYONE WILL BE GETTING NEW SHOES?

YES. WE'LL HAND THEM ALL OUT IN THE MORNING.

THESE SKITS ARE REALLY GREAT, CESAR. THAT AND THE POLITICAL CARTOONS ABOUT THE MOVEMENT IN THE PAPERS.

YEAH, THEY'RE LIFTING EVERYONE'S SPIRITS QUITE A BIT.

IT'S MORE THAN THAT.

MANY OF OUR MEMBERS CAN'T READ. THEY HAD TO LEAVE SCHOOL TO WORK. TO SUPPORT THEIR FAMILIES.

YOU DON'T HAVE TO TELL ME THAT. I KNOW THAT ALL TOO WELL.

THAT'S RIGHT. YOU LEFT SCHOOL AT FOURTEEN, DIDN'T YOU?

FIFTEEN. TO WORK IN THE FIELDS FULL-TIME. MY FAMILY NEEDED THE MONEY.

THAT COULDN'T HAVE BEEN EASY.

IT WASN'T. AND CONDITIONS IN THE FIELDS HAVEN'T GOTTEN MUCH BETTER SINCE THEN.

EXCUSE ME, CESAR.

42

El Plan de Delano

"El Plan de Delano" was a speech that Cesar wrote together with Luis Valdez, an American playwright, actor, and film director. It was inspired by "El Plan de Ayala," a speech written by the followers of Emiliano Zapata, who was a leading figure in the Mexican Revolution. "El Plan de Delano" was meant to be read every night of the march to help unify the marchers and remind them of their purpose to fight for workers' rights. Cesar felt it was important that the speech was focused on actions and not words. The speech spoke of uniting, striking, and overcoming the injustices the farmworkers experienced.

The speech was completed just days before the march to Sacramento.

44

47

Dolores Huerta

Dolores Clara Fernández was born on April 10, 1930, in Dawson, New Mexico, but spent most of her early childhood in Stockton, California.

Her father, Juan Fernández, was a farmworker, but she was raised mostly by a single mother, Alicia Chavez Fernández, whose community work and independent spirit inspired Dolores to get more involved in activism.

Dolores cofounded the National Farm Workers Association along with Cesar in 1962. Her determination and experience as a member of multiple organizations, including the Girl Scouts, helped her secure government programs like Aid to Families with Dependent Children (AFDC) along with disability protection for farmworkers in California.

In 2008, President Barack Obama adopted a personal quote of Dolores's, "Sí, se puede," which became a popular mantra for his campaign. It means, "Yes, we can," or "Yes, it can be done." In 2012, President Obama awarded Dolores the Presidential Medal of Freedom, the highest award given to a civilian in the United States.

DOWN THE ROAD A WAYS

CESAR, WHEN WE STOPPED AT THE LAST FARM, THE TEAM AHEAD LEFT US A MESSAGE. SCHENLEY CALLED. THEY TRIED SEVERAL TIMES, BUT THERE ISN'T EXACTLY A PHONE OUT HERE.

THEY WANT TO TALK TO YOU.

REALLY?

THEY DO?

CESAR, THEY WANT TO SETTLE THIS.

ALL RIGHT. WHEN WE GET TO STOCKTON, I'LL CALL THEM.

STOCKTON

WELCOME TO STOCKTON

HUELGA

HUE

ESQUIRC   PATRÓN

Conclusion

In August 1966, the NFWA united with another union, the Agricultural Workers Organizing Committee. The two unions became known as the United Farm Workers. Uniting these two groups made them much stronger, and not long after, Cesar received a telegram from civil rights leader Dr. Martin Luther King Jr. that said, "Our separate struggles are really one—a struggle for freedom, for dignity, and for humanity."

The grape strike went on for over five years. While many agreements were signed, progress was slow. A lot of farmworkers were still left unprotected and grew impatient. In fact, some workers felt that fighting back physically was the only answer. This caused a divide within the union. Cesar, committed to nonviolence, decided to do what Gandhi did: On February 15, 1968, he began a hunger strike to show that violence was not the answer. This meant that he would go without food and only drink water until the violence stopped. The strike was very tough. With every day that passed, he grew weaker. He lost thirty-five pounds! Cesar's wife, Helen Chavez, was worried for his life. Doctors begged him to stop. But the union members heard Cesar's message: All talk of violence stopped from then on, and after twenty-five days, he ended the strike.

In 1969, Cesar expanded his boycott of the grapes into Canada.

He asked stores to stop buying grapes grown in California. By 1970, the farm owners were losing so much money that they agreed to strike a deal with the UFW: They signed contracts that recognized the union and agreed to better working conditions for the farmworkers.

In April 1993, Cesar Chavez passed away at the age of sixty-six. The impact that Cesar had on farmworkers, migrant workers, and people of all kinds is recognized around the world today. After his death, he was awarded the Presidential Medal of Freedom by President Bill Clinton and the Águila Azteca (the Aztec Eagle), the highest award given to foreign citizens by the Mexican government.

Timeline of Cesar Chavez's Life

1927 — Cesar Estrada Chavez is born on March 31 near Yuma, Arizona

1938 — Cesar's family leaves Arizona and moves to California to begin work as migrant farmworkers

1948 — Marries Helen Fabela on October 22

1955 — Meets Dolores Huerta

1962 — Cesar and Dolores form the National Farm Workers Association

— The NFWA flag is revealed at the first meeting for the National Farm Workers Association

1965 — Agrees to join the strike against the grape growers in the San Joaquin Valley

1966 — Leads a 340-mile march from Delano to California's capitol building in Sacramento in March and April

1968 — Fasts for twenty-five days in protest against violent farmworker actions

1970 — Grape growers sign contracts on July 29, ending the five-year grape strike

1988 — Fasts for thirty-six days in protest against pesticide use

1993 — Dies in San Luis, Arizona, on April 23

Bibliography

*Books for young readers

Bratt, Peter, dir. *Dolores.* 5 Stick Films, 2017.

Brunner, Borgna. "Timeline: Cesar Chavez." February 28, 2017. **Infoplease.com.** https://www.infoplease.com/history/hispanic-heritage/timeline-cesar-chavez.

"Cesar Chavez and the Farmworker Movement." May 29, 2014. *University of California Television*, YouTube video, 51:35. https://www.youtube.com/watch?v=-2_3mWGl5ws&t=672s.

Fuentes, Ed. "How One Flag Went From Representing Farmworkers to Flying for the Entire Latino Community." April 2, 2014. **TakePart. com.** http://www.takepart.com/article/2014/04/02/cultural-history-ufw-flag/.

García, Mario T. *The Gospel of César Chávez: My Faith in Action.* Lanham, MD: Sheed & Ward, 2007.

*Rau, Dana Meachen. *Who Was Cesar Chavez?* New York: Penguin Workshop, 2017.

Valdez, Louis. "Commentary of Luis Valdez: The Plan of Delano." *Farmworker Movement Documentation Project: Presented by the UC San Diego Library.* https://libraries.ucsd.edu/farmworkermovement/essays/essays/Plan%20of%20Delano.pdf.

ABOUT THE CREATORS

Terry Blas is an illustrator and writer based in Portland, Oregon. His auto-bio comics *You Say Latino* and *You Say LatinX* were featured on NPR, OPB, Vox.com, and Cosmo.com. Terry's work has appeared in the comics The Amazing World of Gumball, Adventure Time, and Steven Universe. His first graphic novel, *Dead Weight: Murder at Camp Bloom*, was named by YALSA as a 2019 Quick Pick for Reluctant Young Readers. His second graphic novel, *Hotel Dare*, is an all-ages, fantasy epic inspired by his childhood in Mexico. His third book, *Lifetime Passes*, will be published by Surely Books.

Mar Julia is an Ignatz Award-nominated cartoonist and illustrator living in Baltimore, Maryland. Their debut graphic novel, *Brownstone*, a collaboration with writer Samuel Teer, is scheduled for release from Versify in 2022.